# Formes
## de coloriage

**Coloring Pages for Kids**



Coloring Pages for Kids
An imprint of Ciparum LLC

Formes de coloriage
© 2017 Ciparum LLC
All rights reserved.
ISBN-10:1-63589-411-5
ISBN-13:978-1-63589-411-0

**Coloring Pages for Kids**

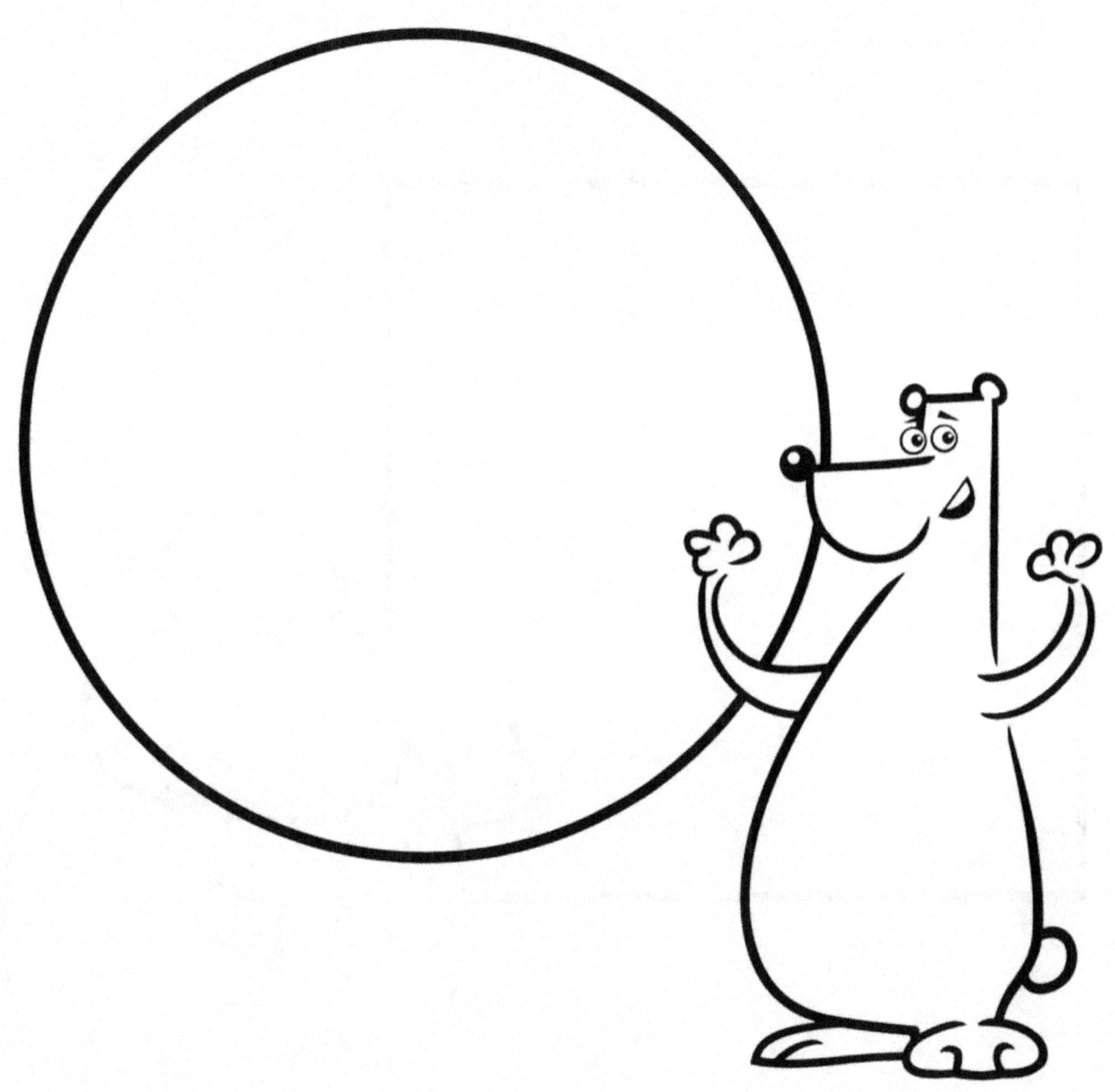

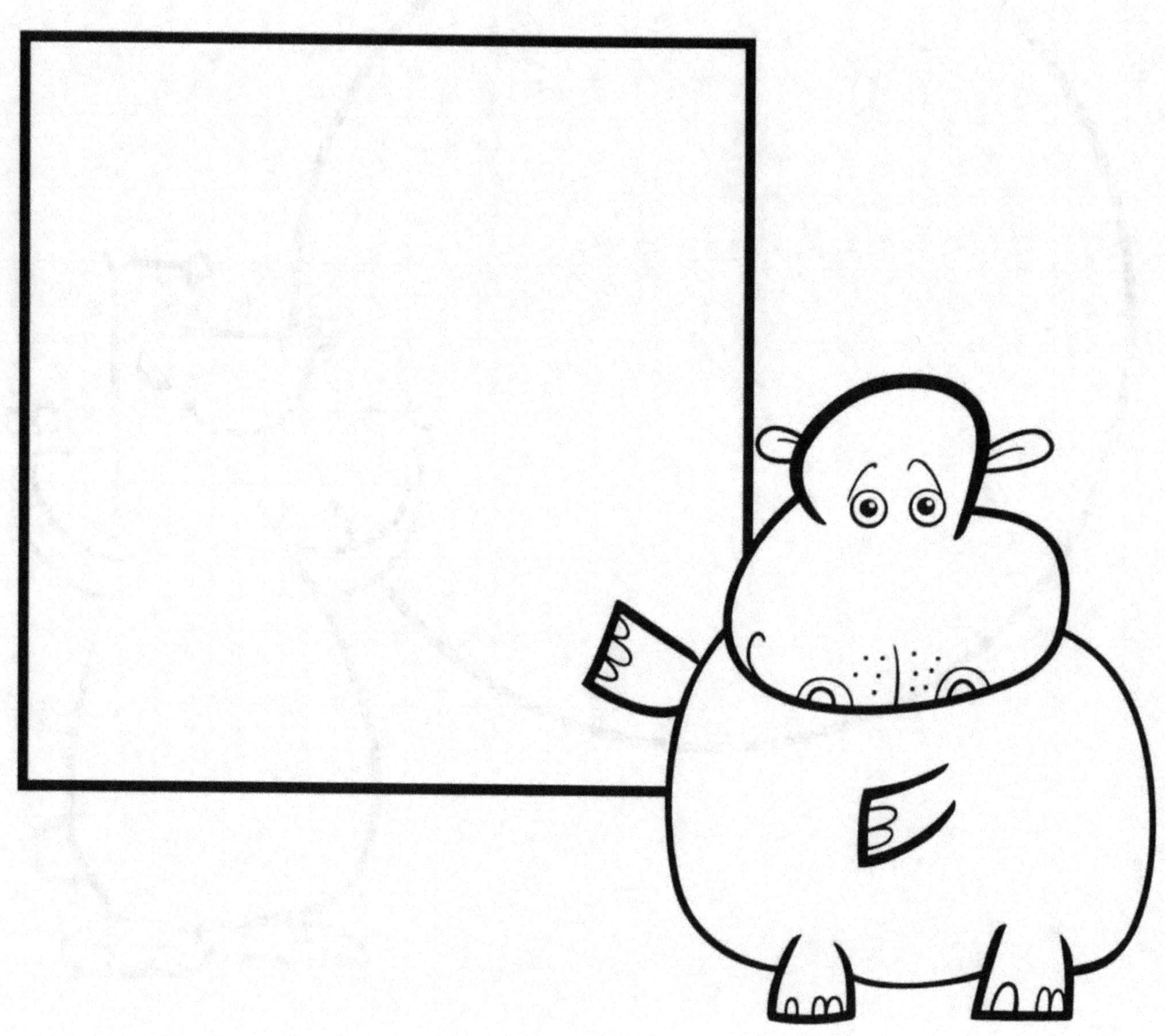

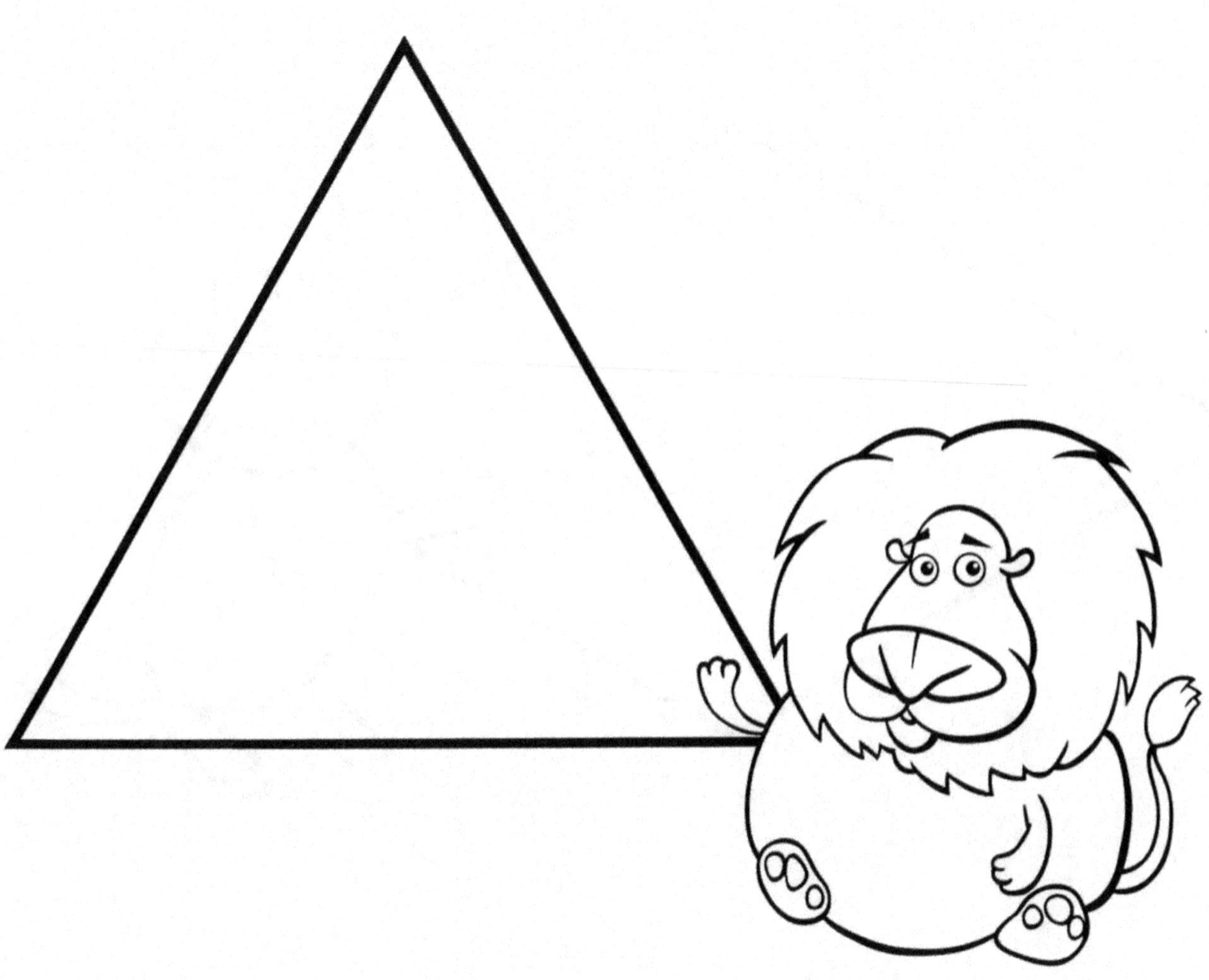

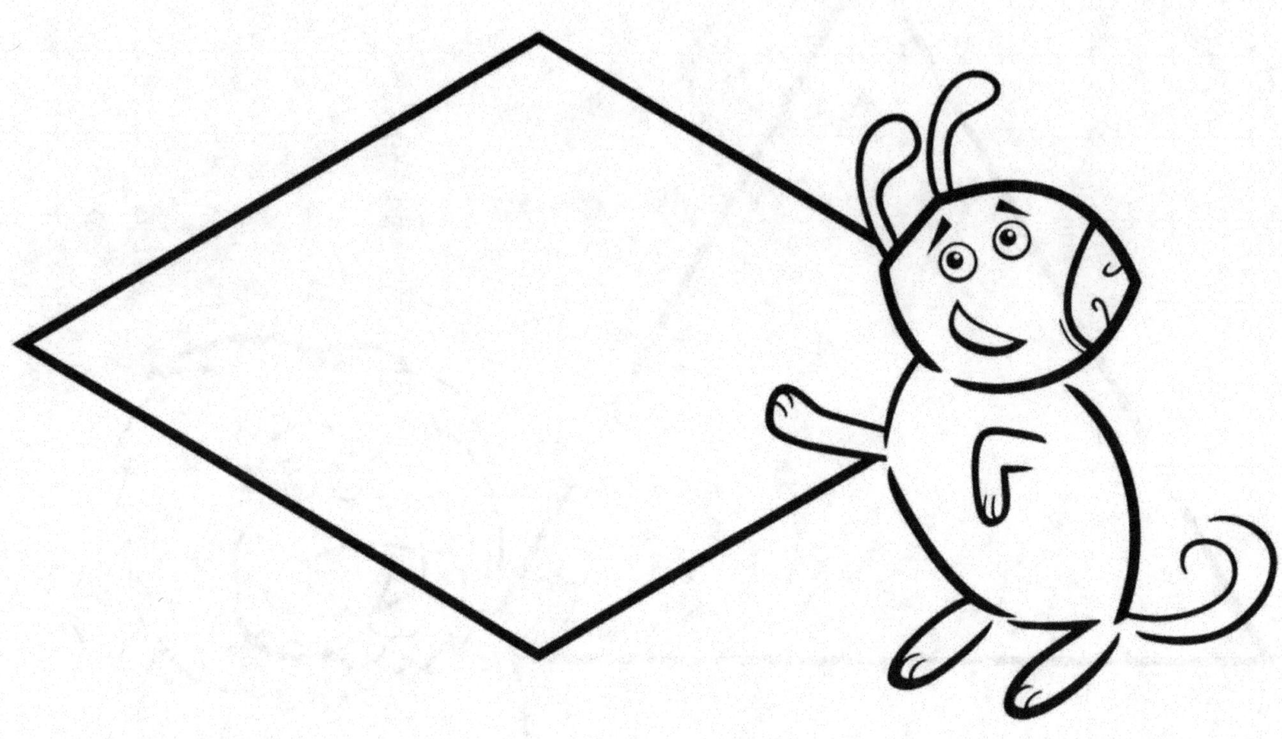

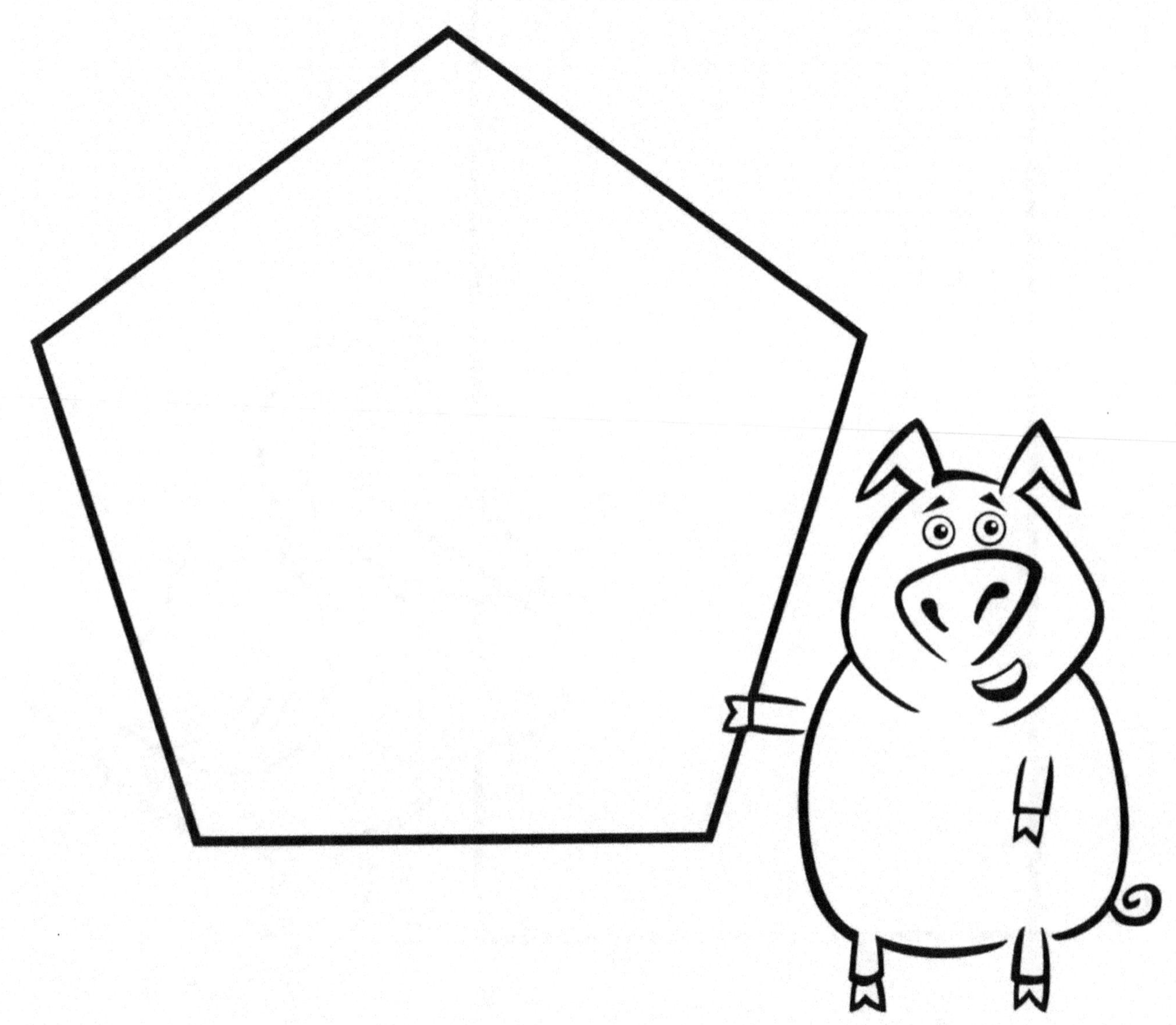

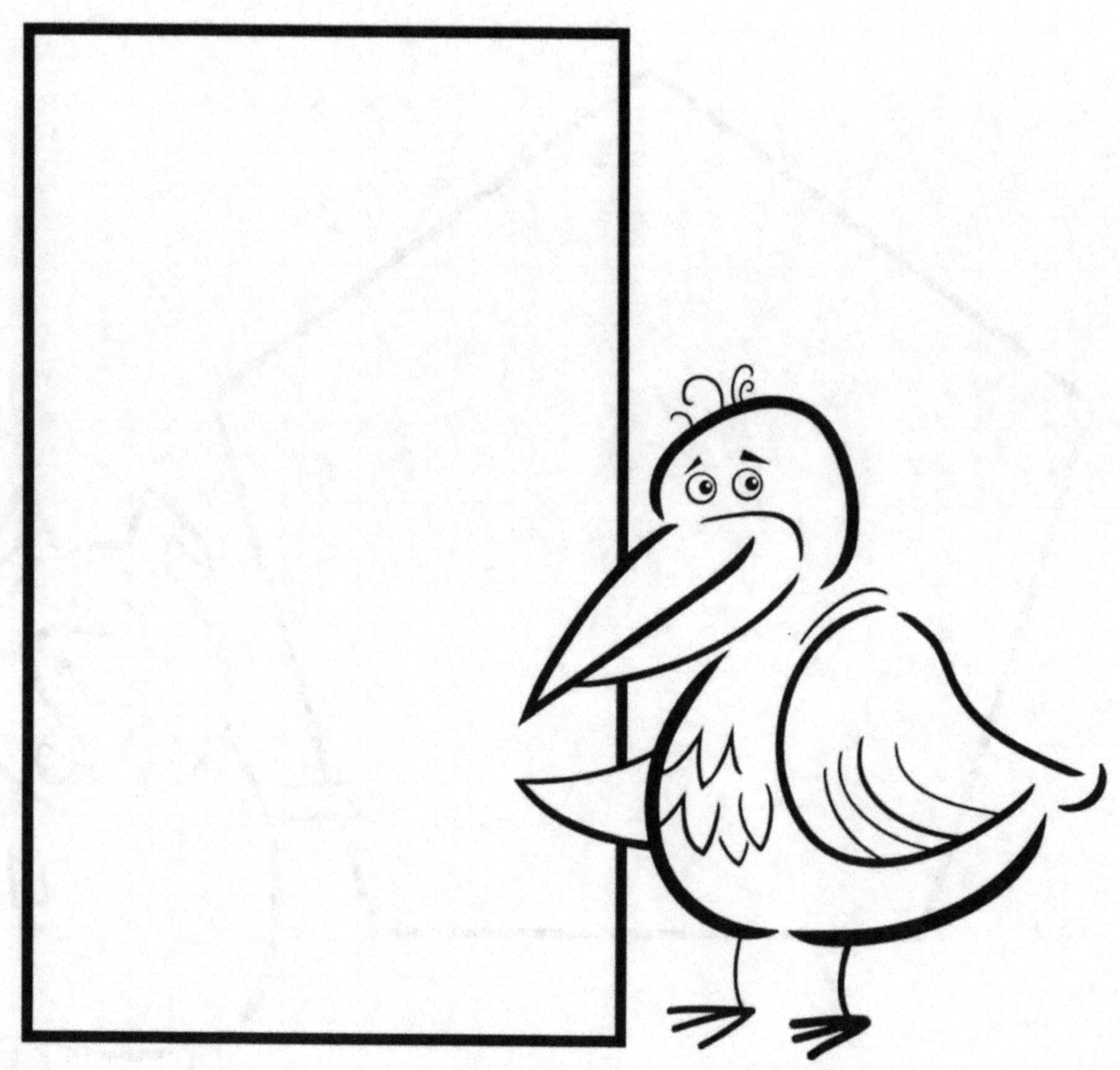

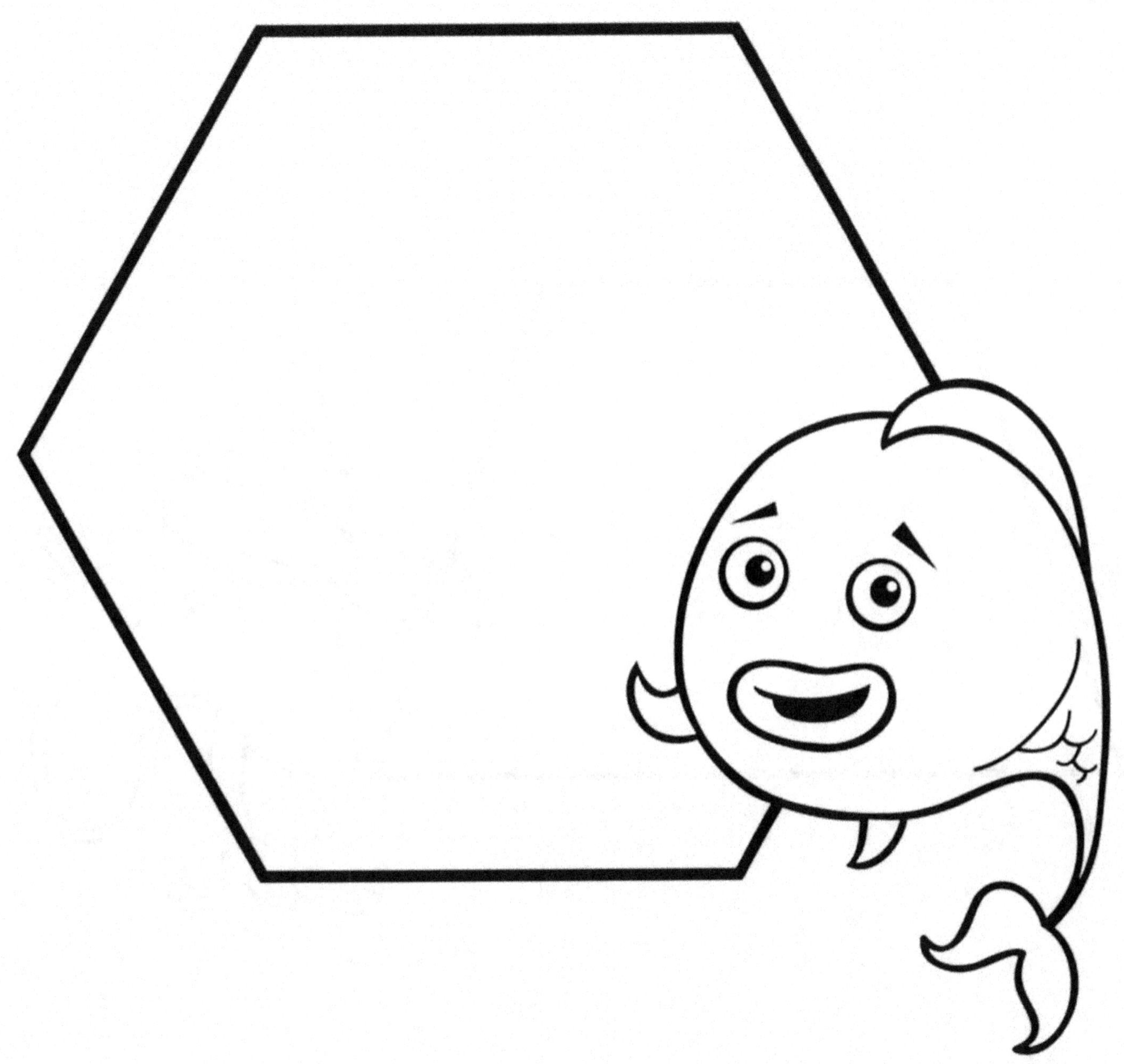

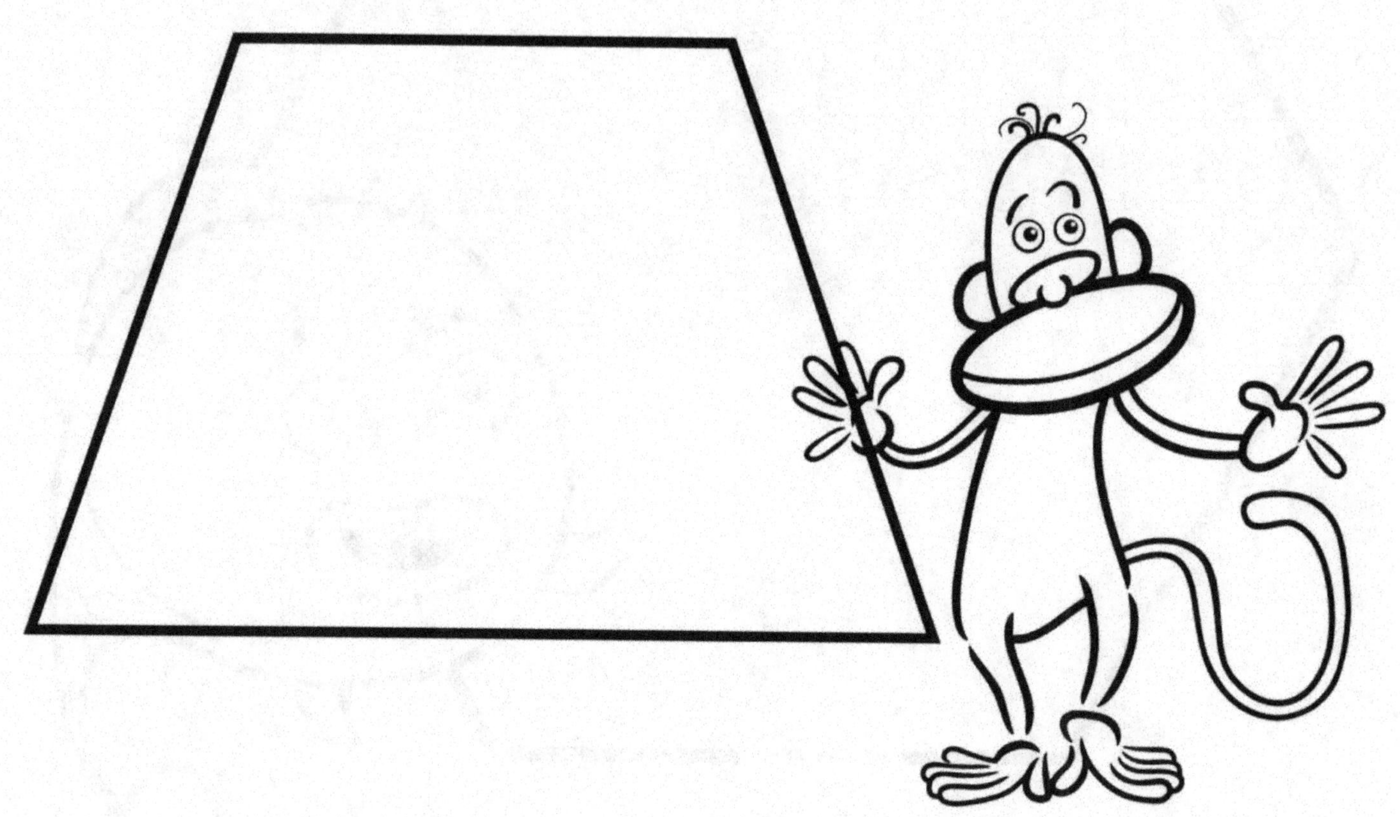

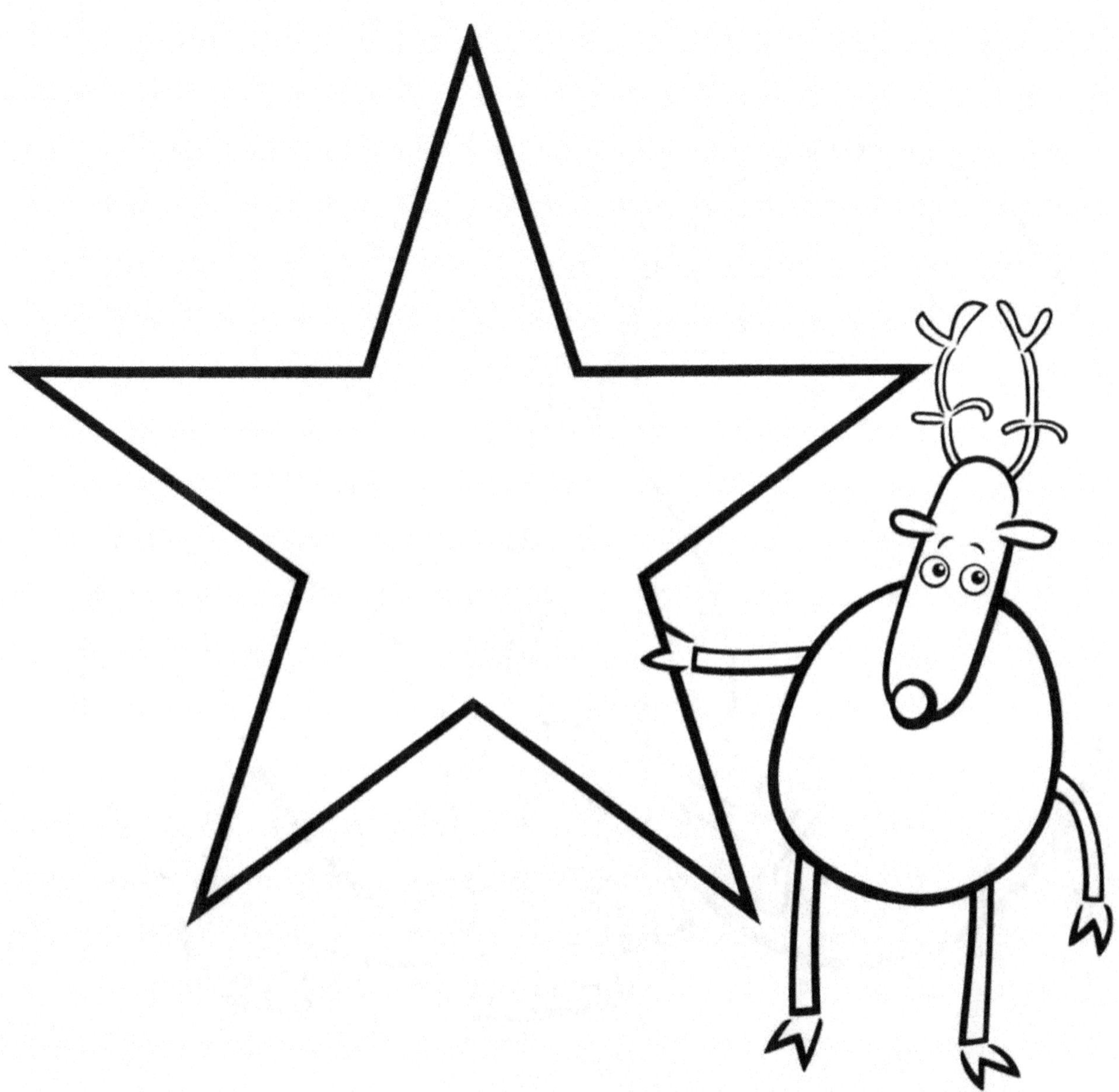

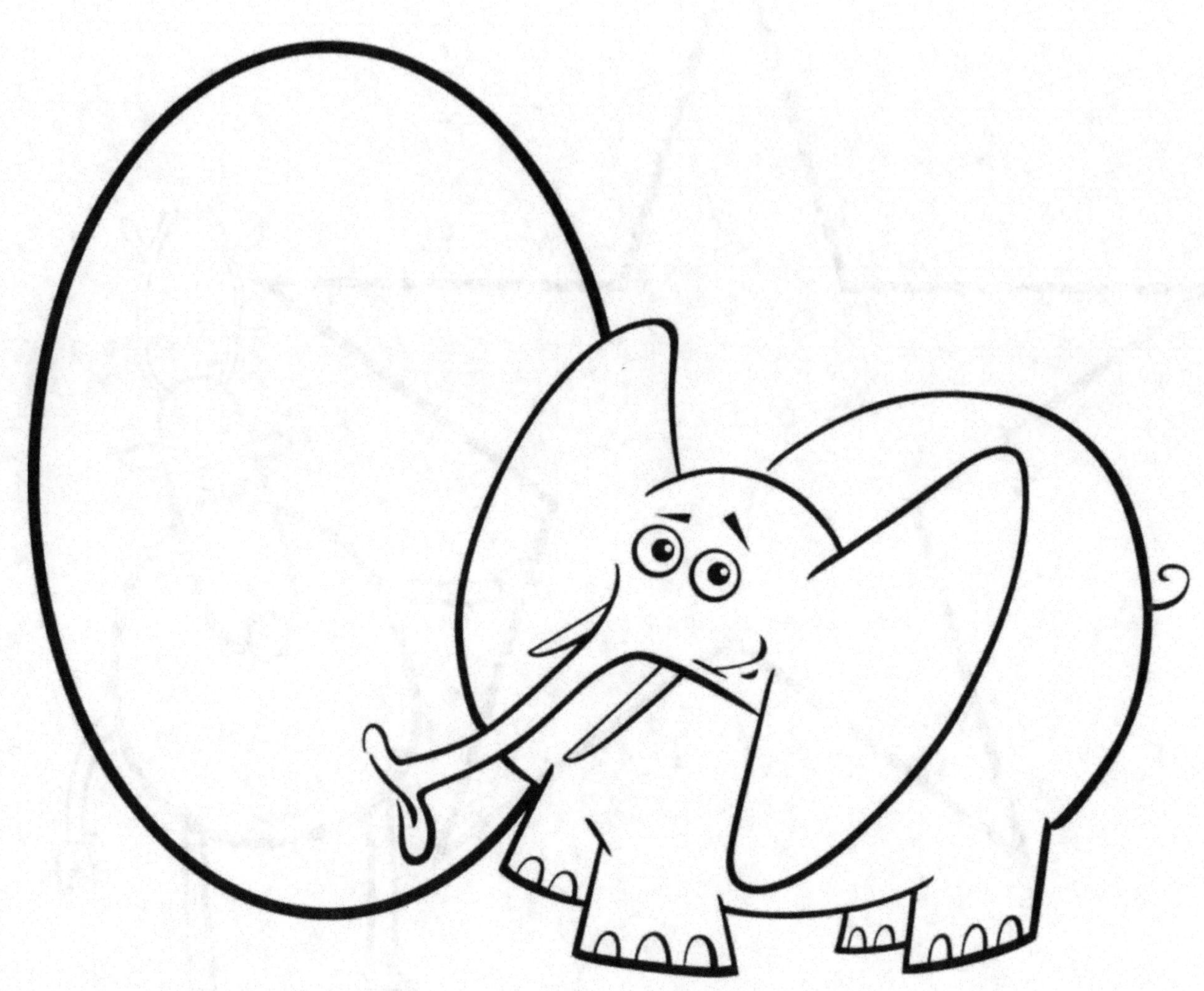

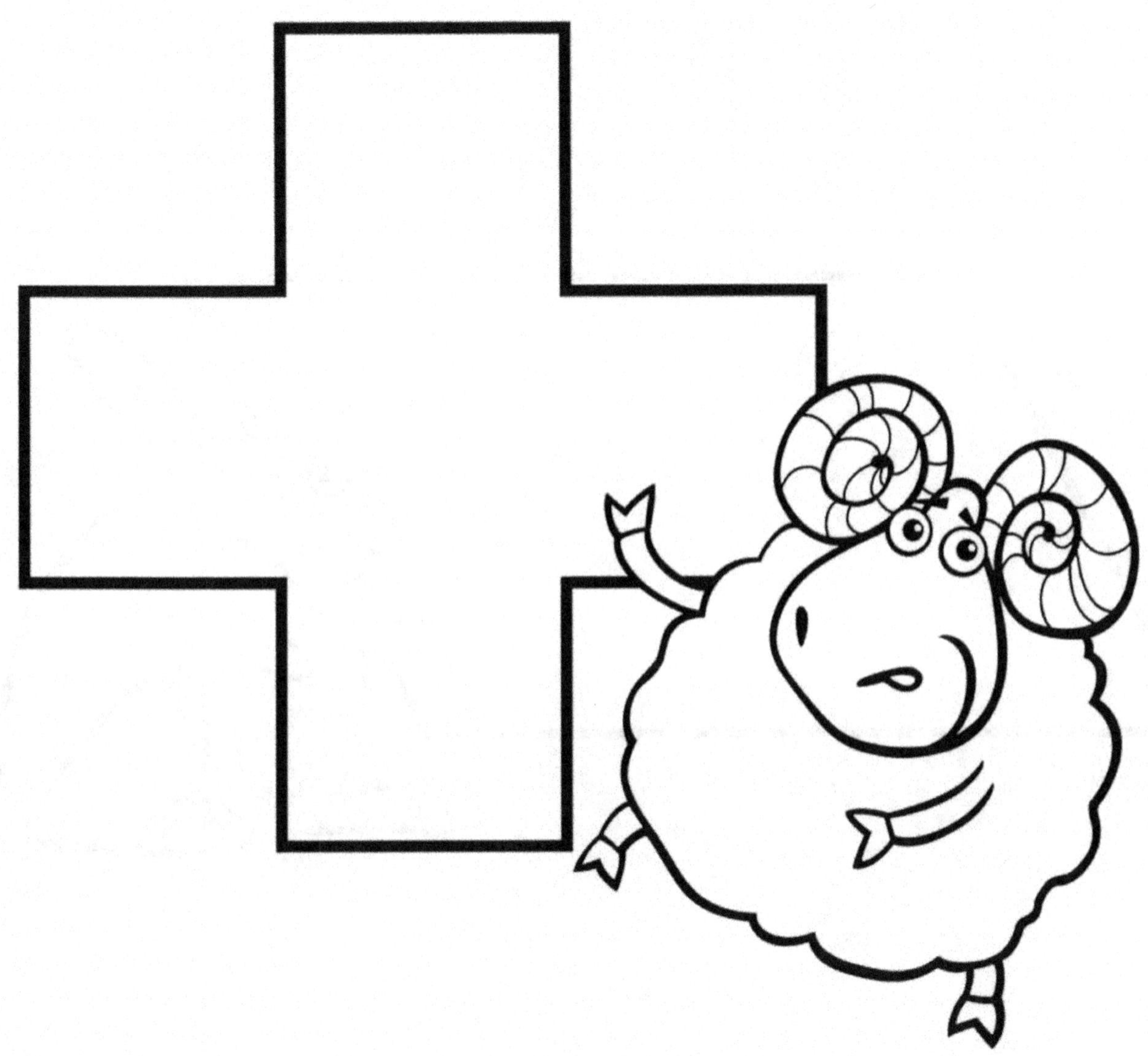

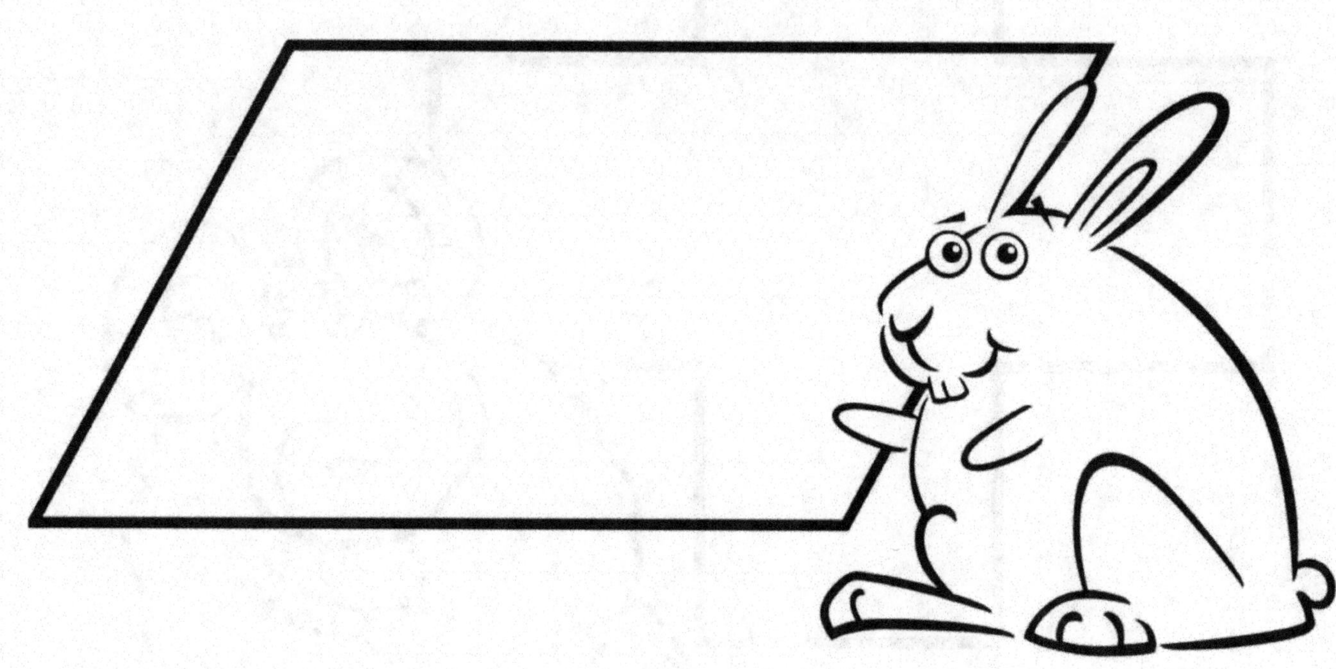

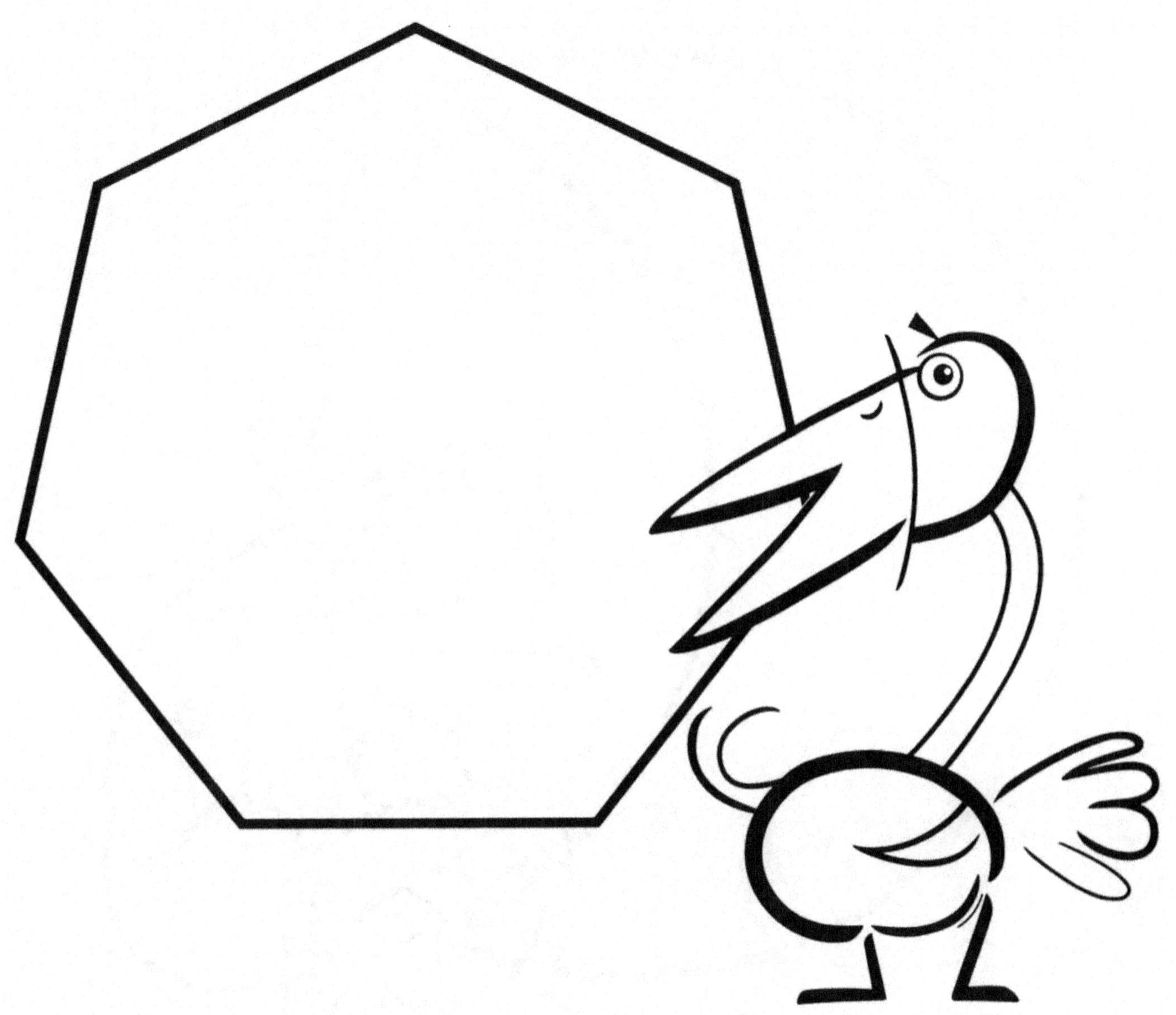

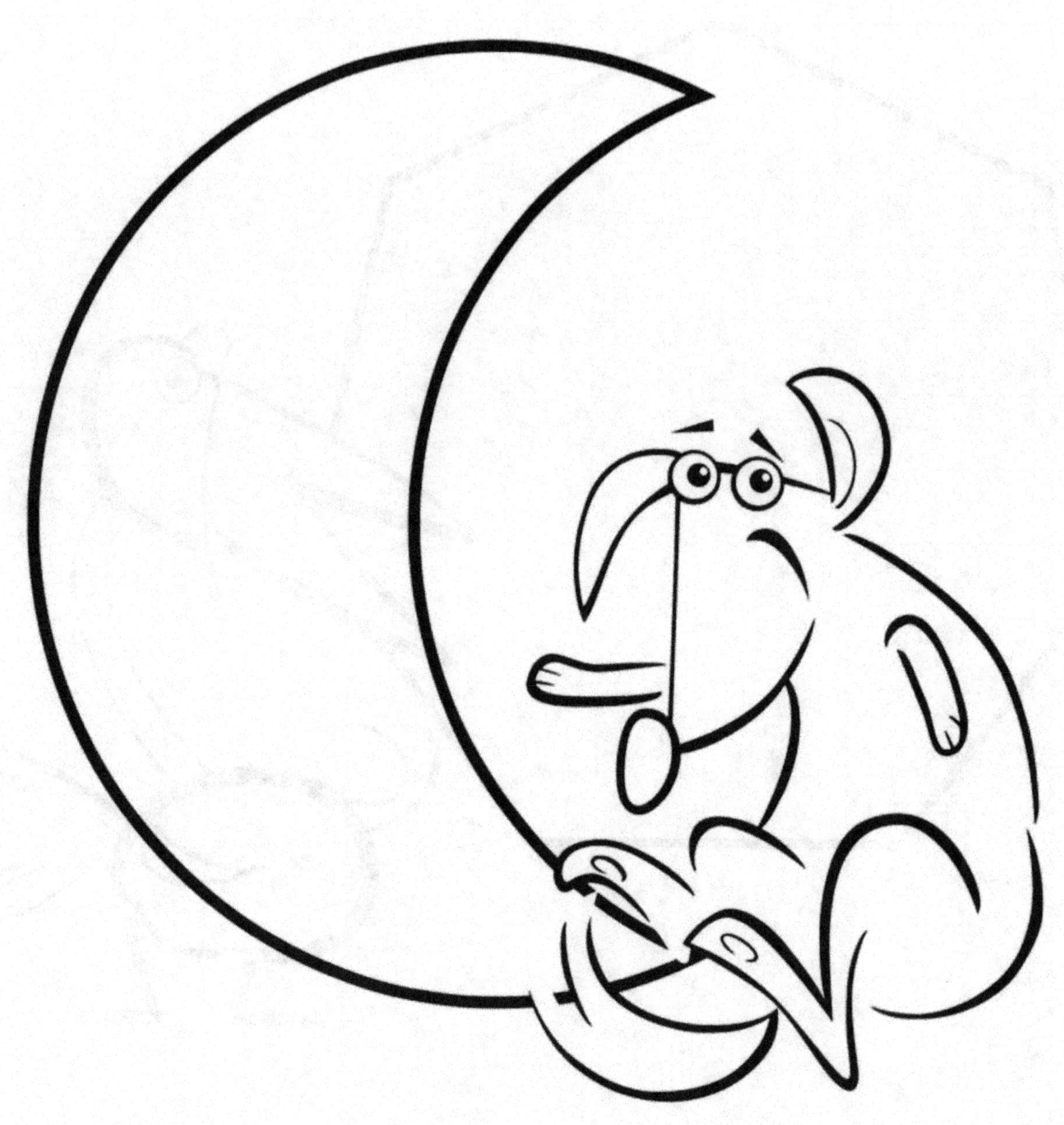

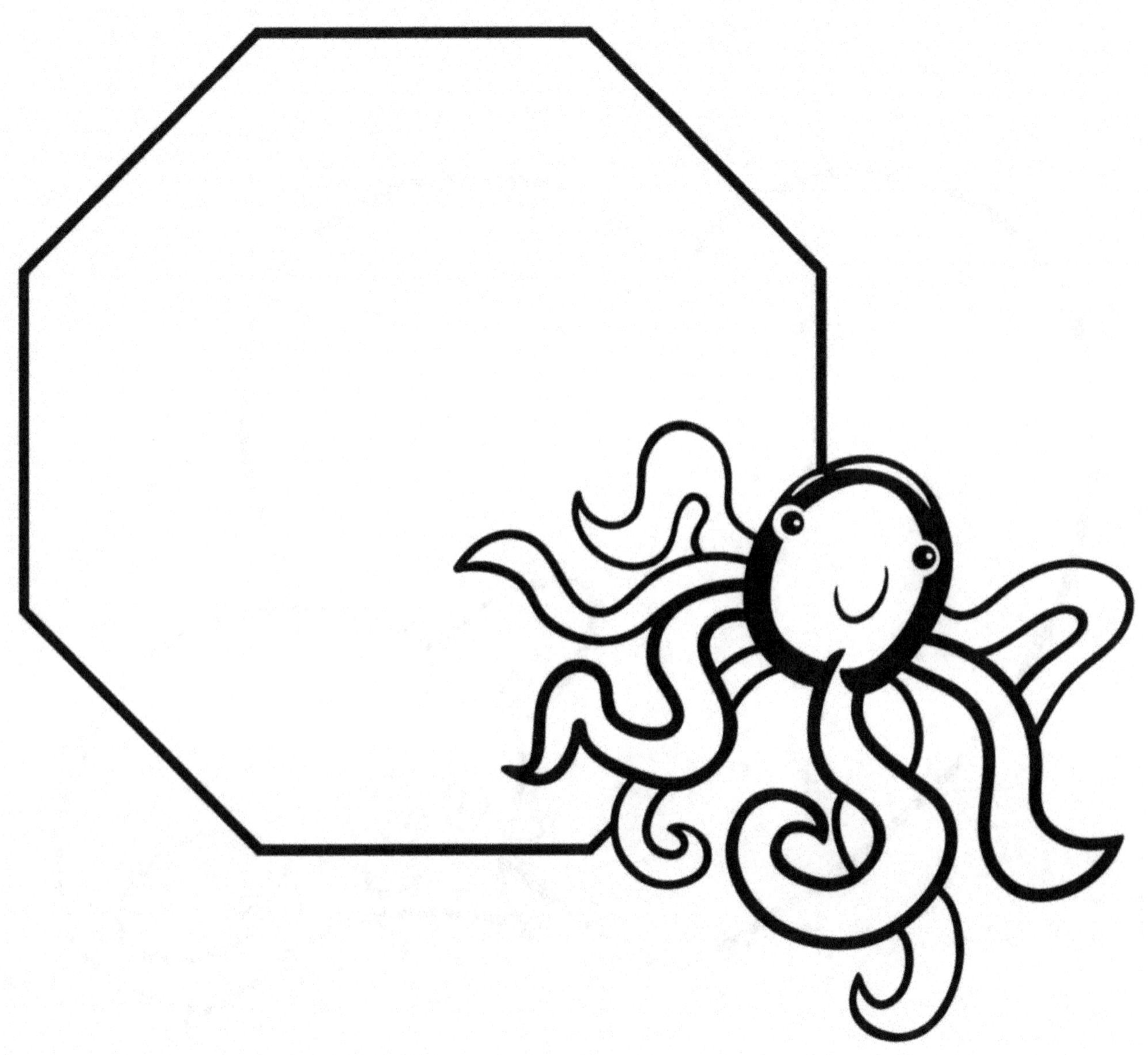

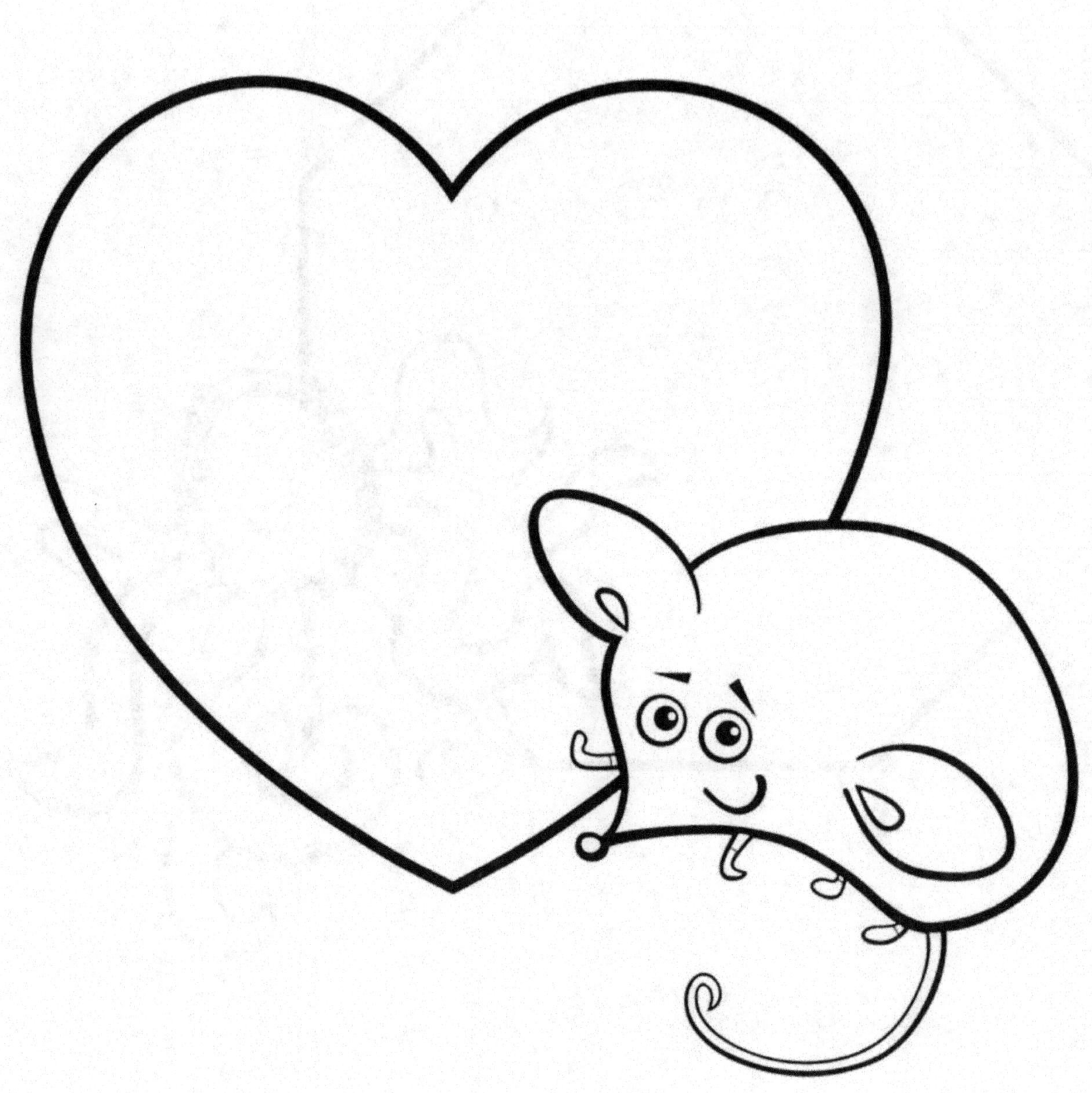

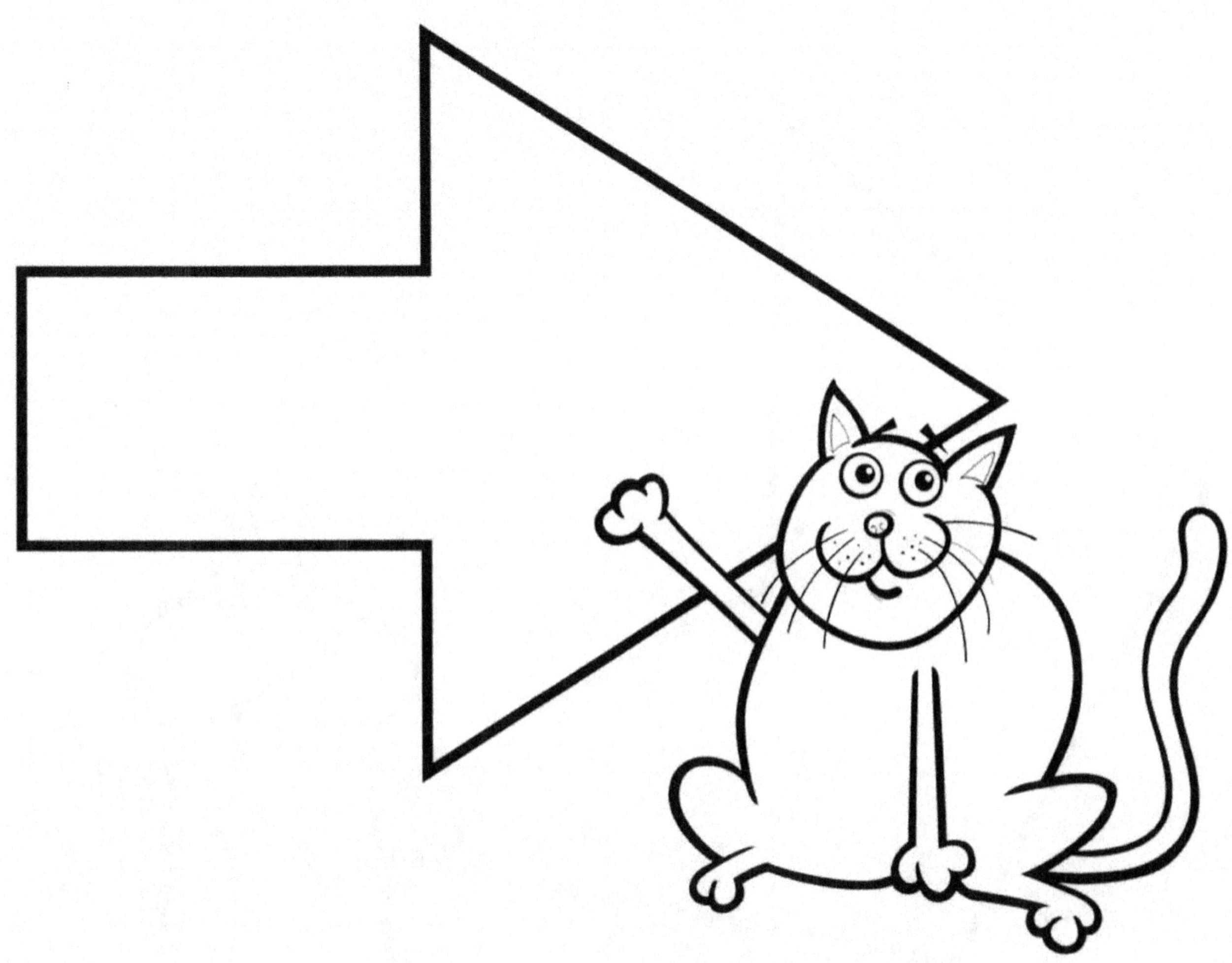

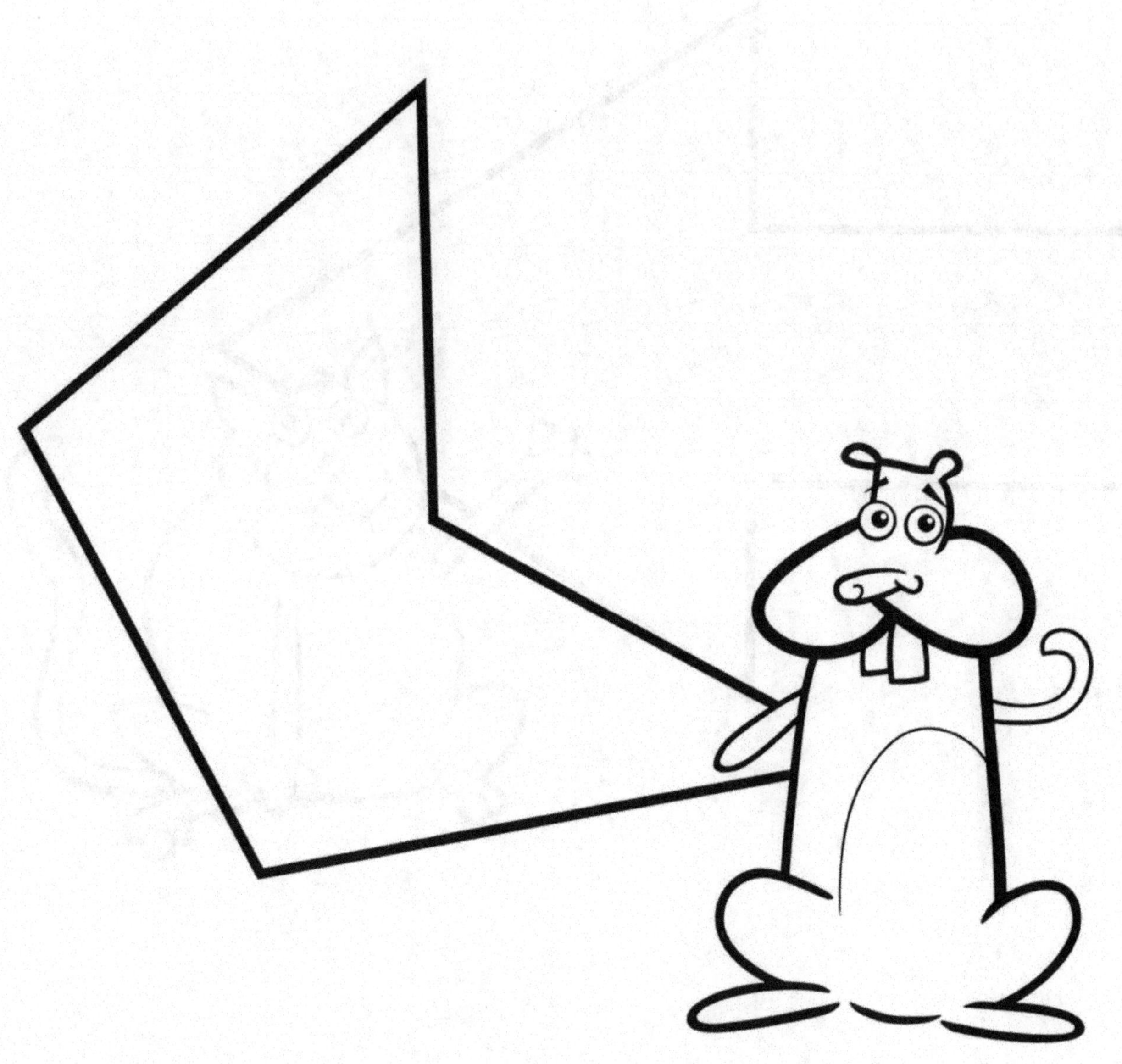

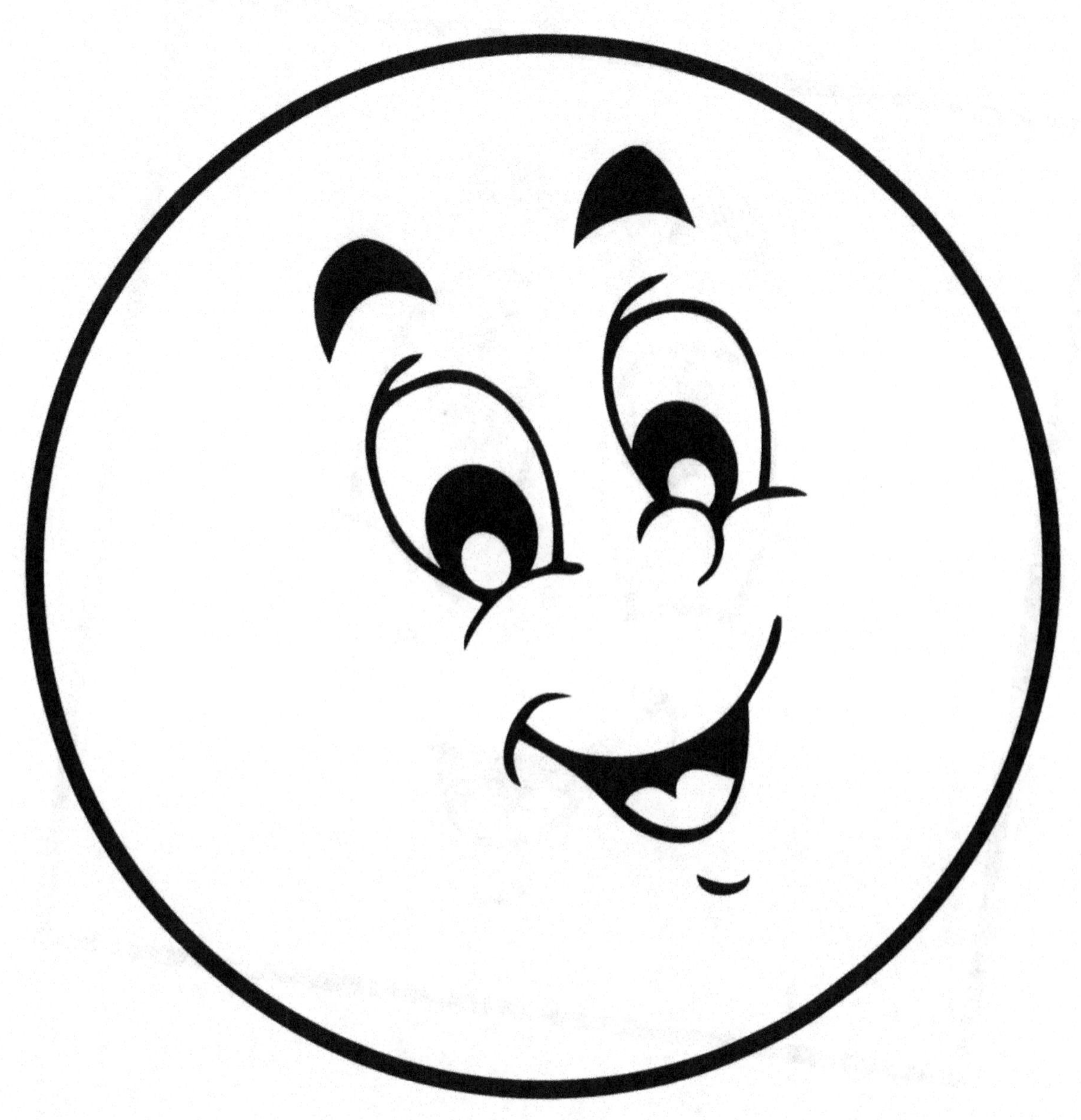

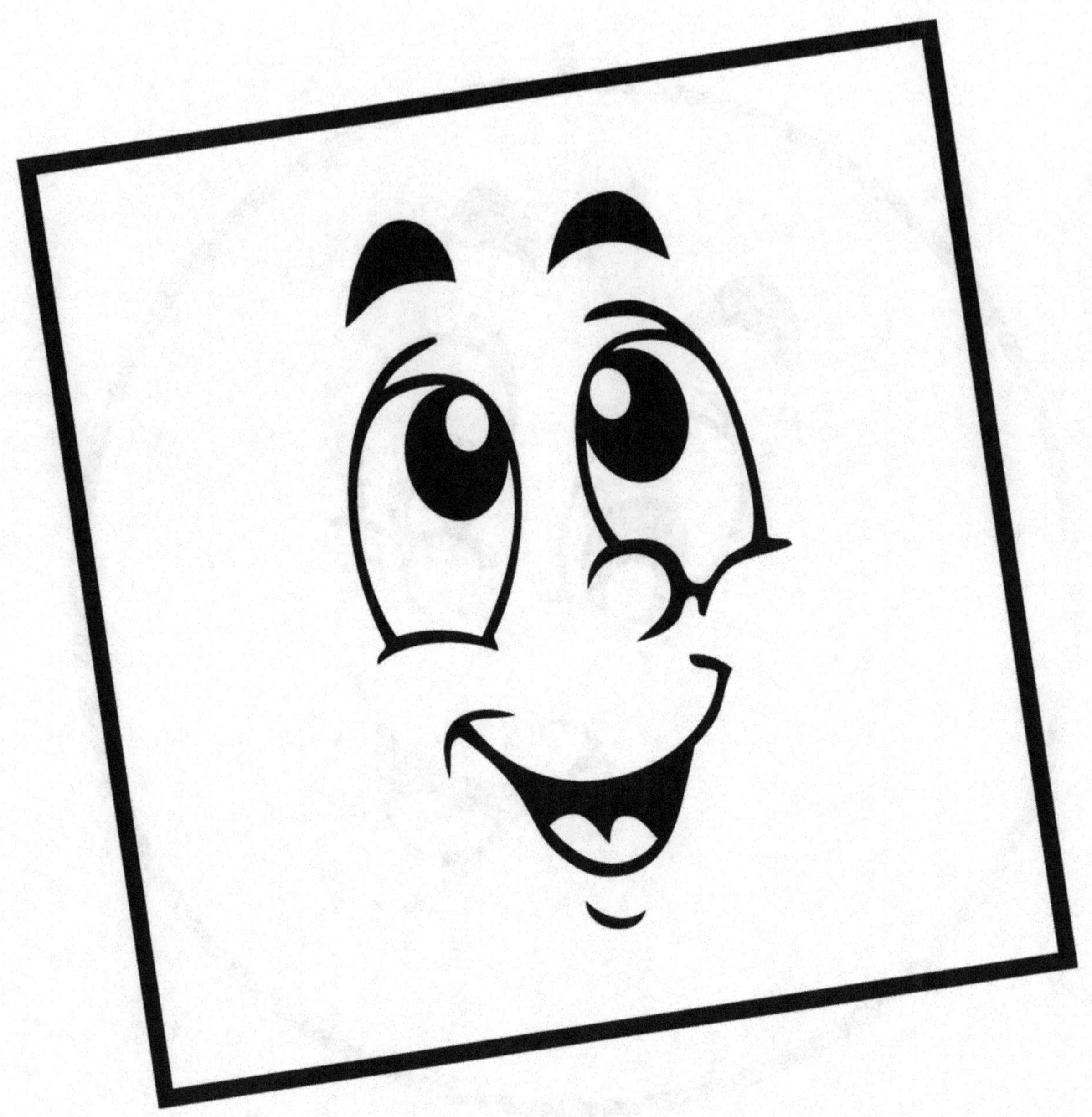

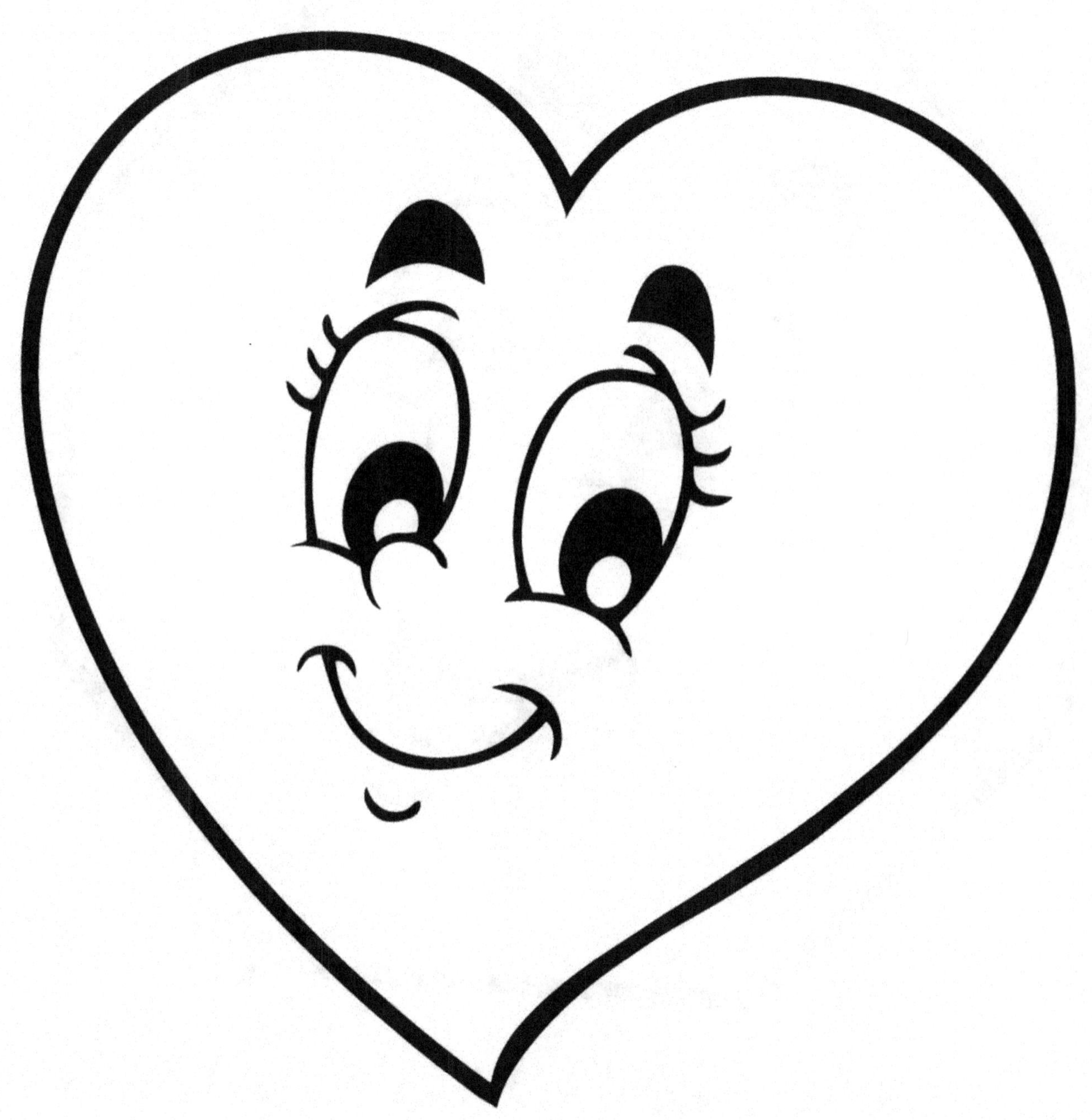

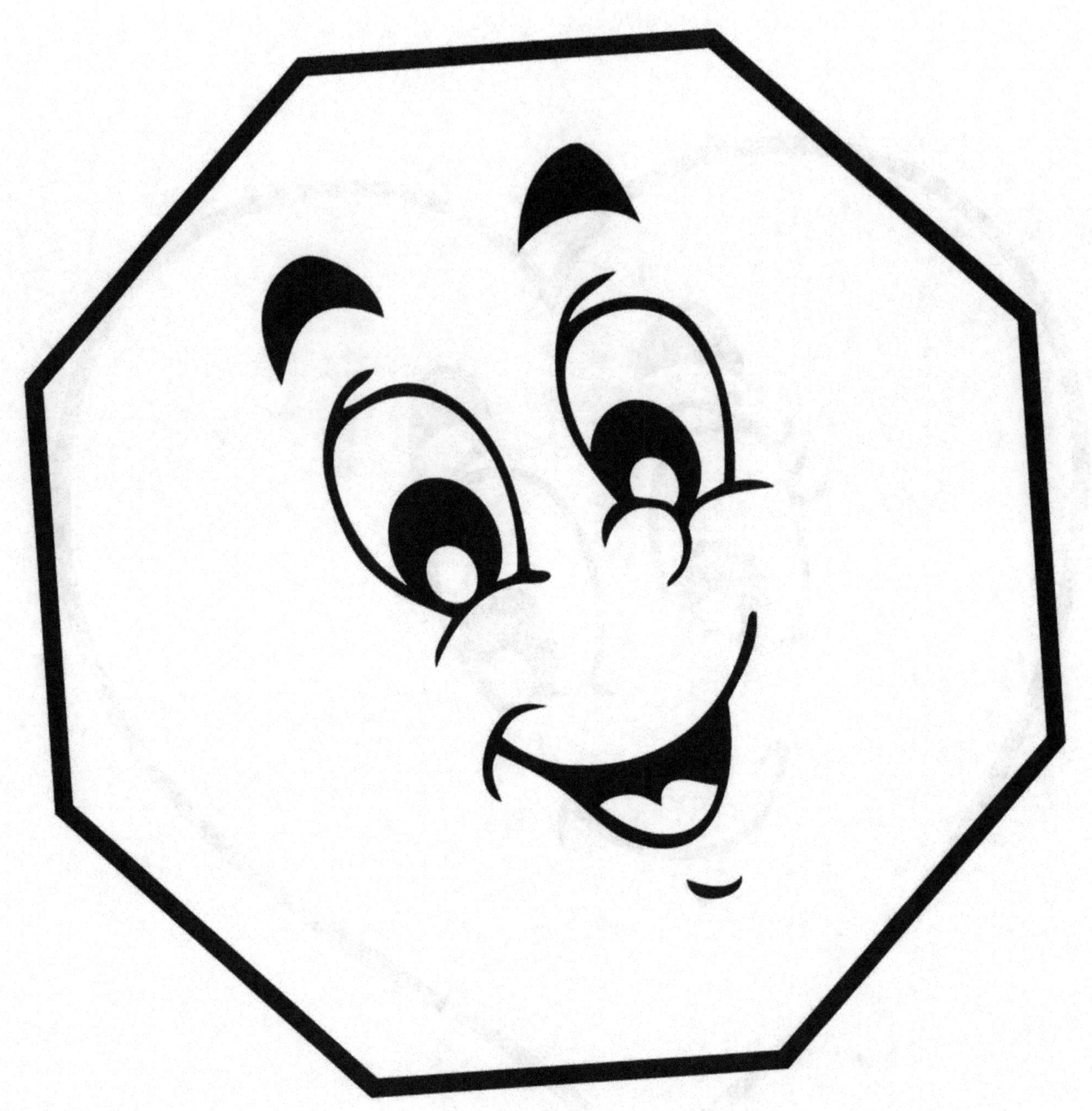

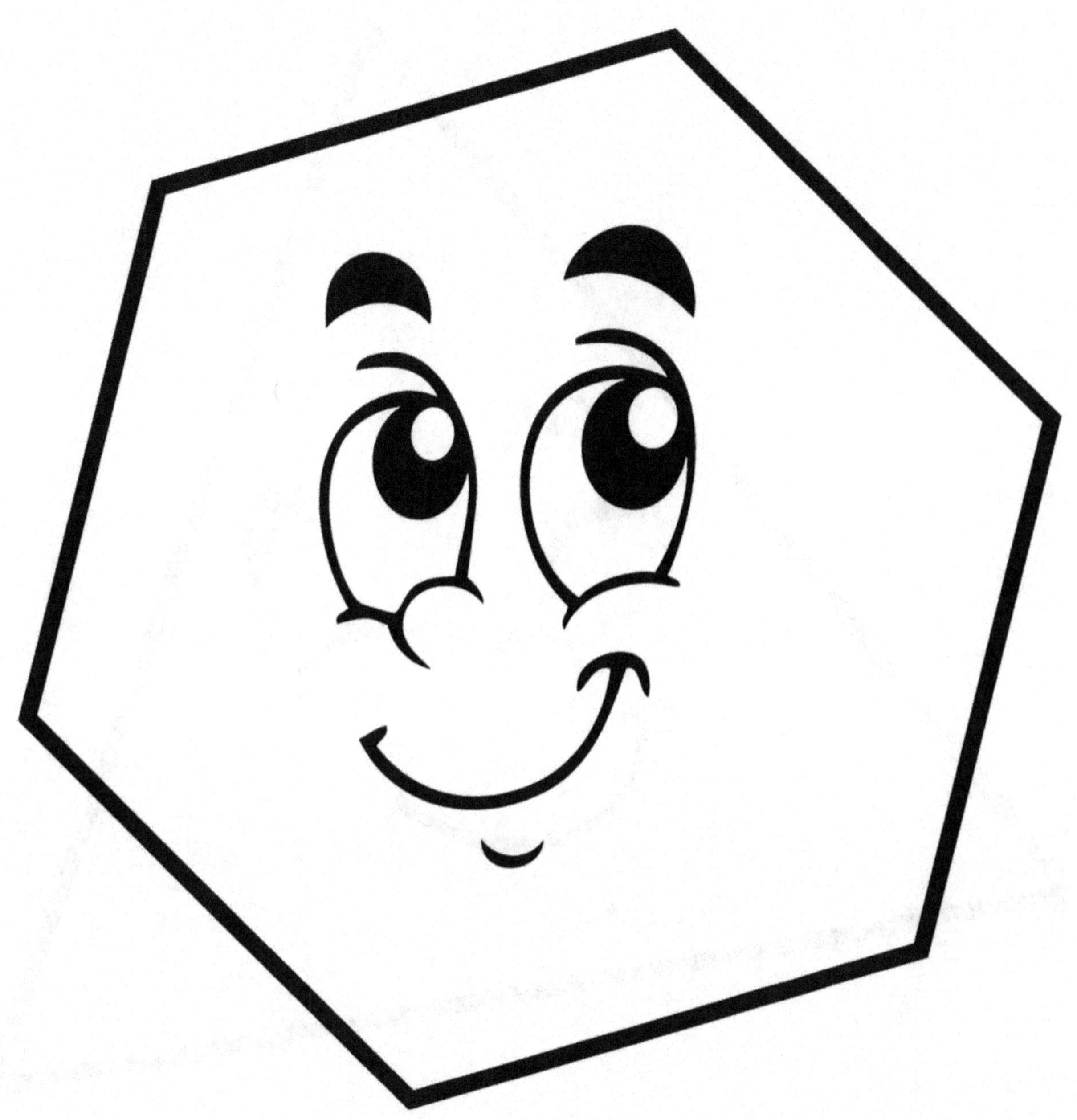

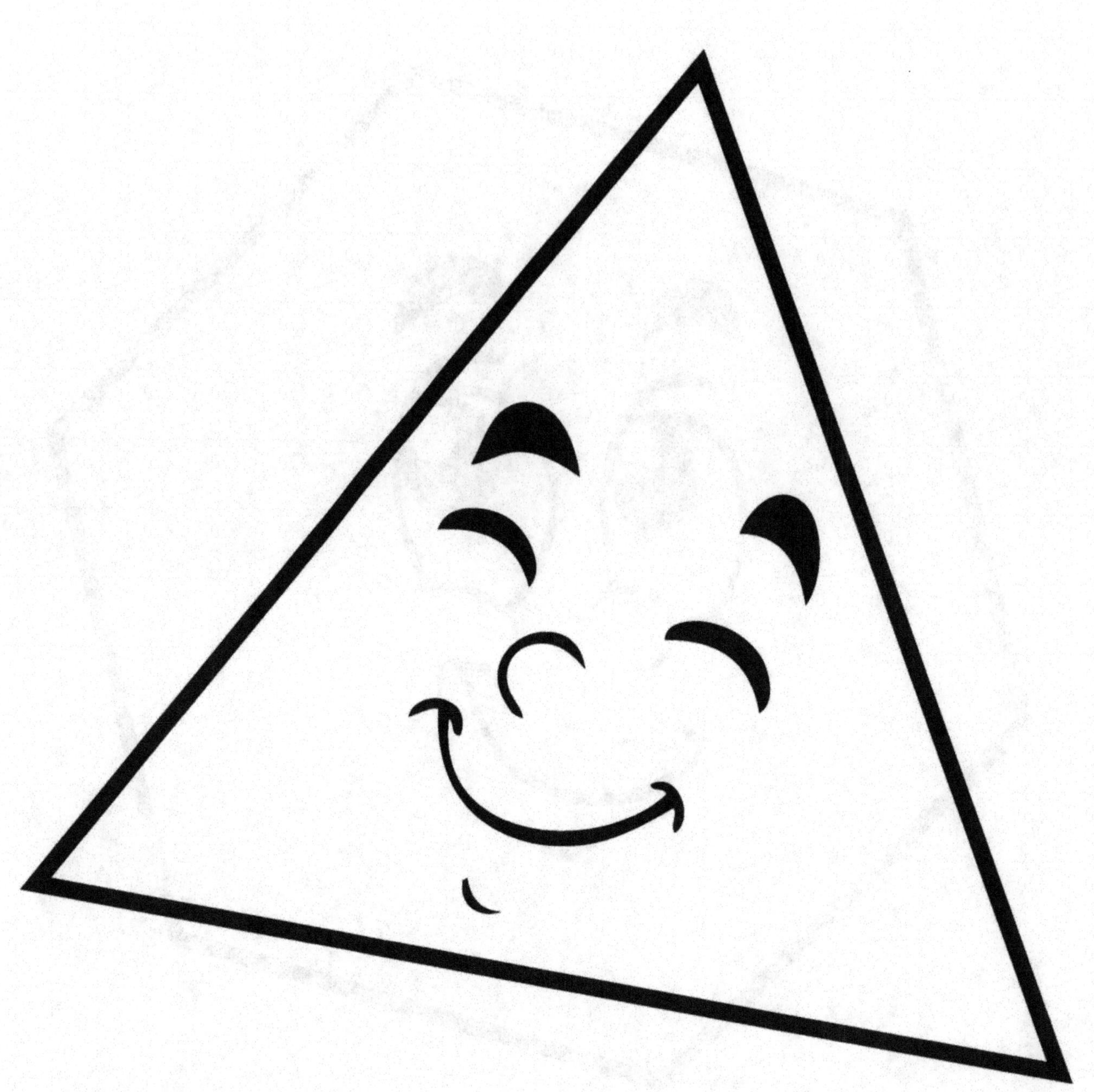

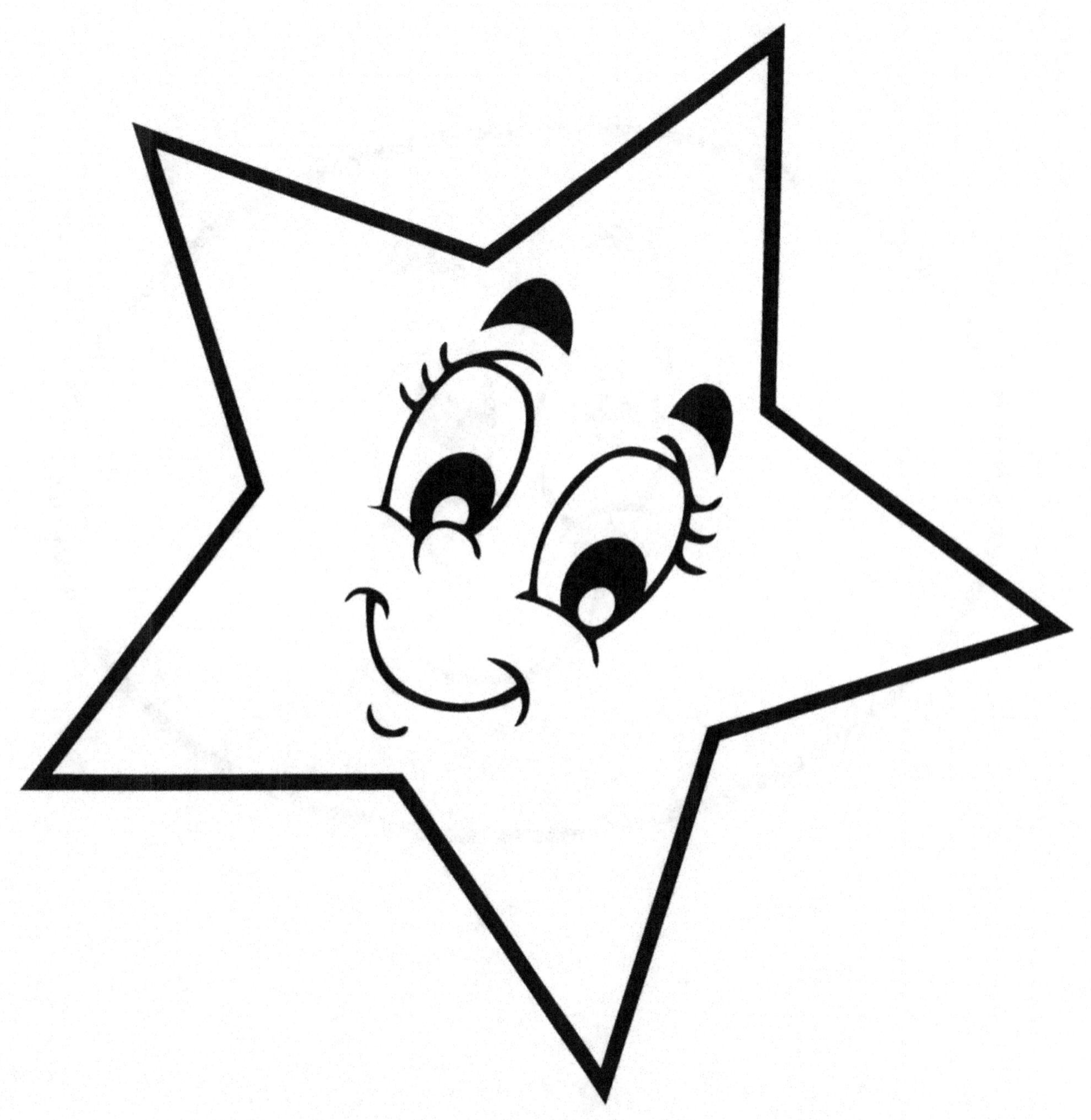

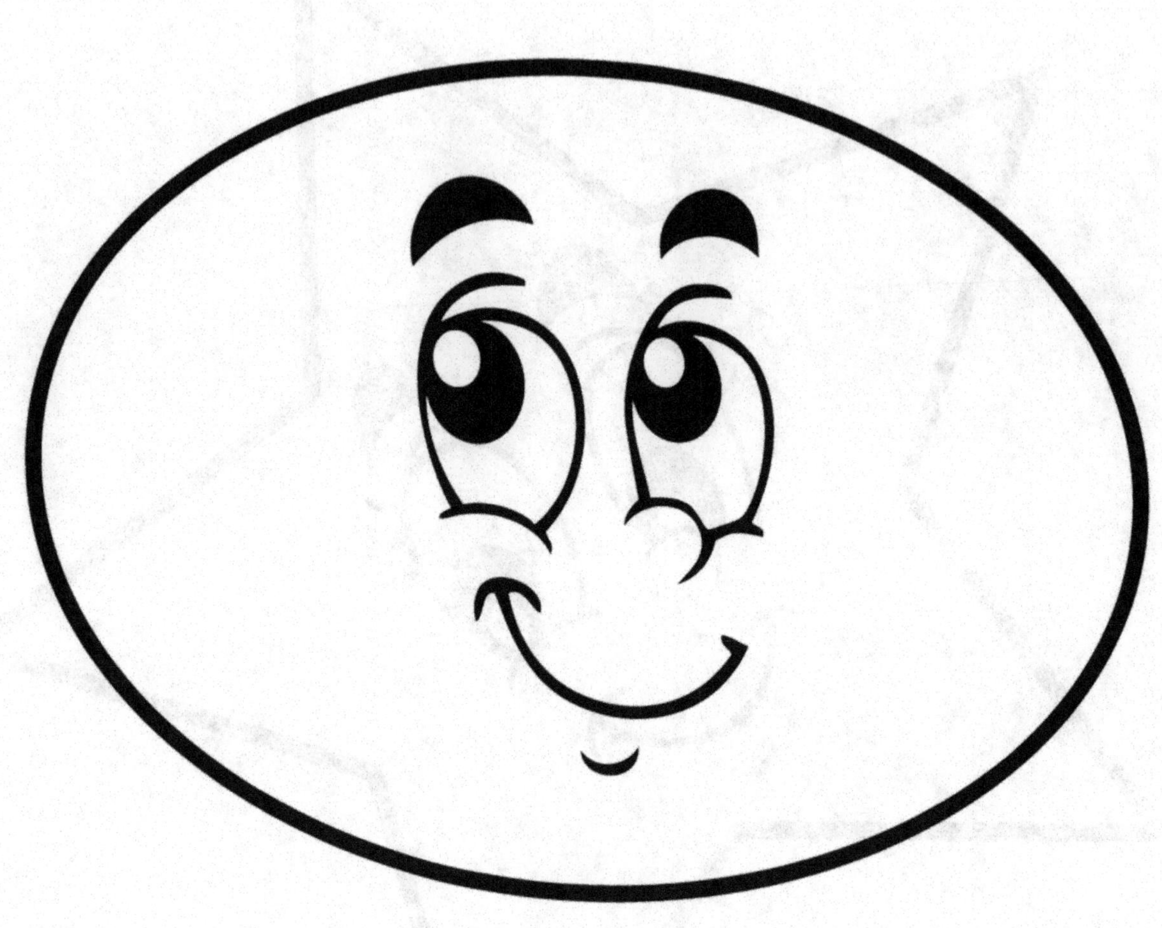

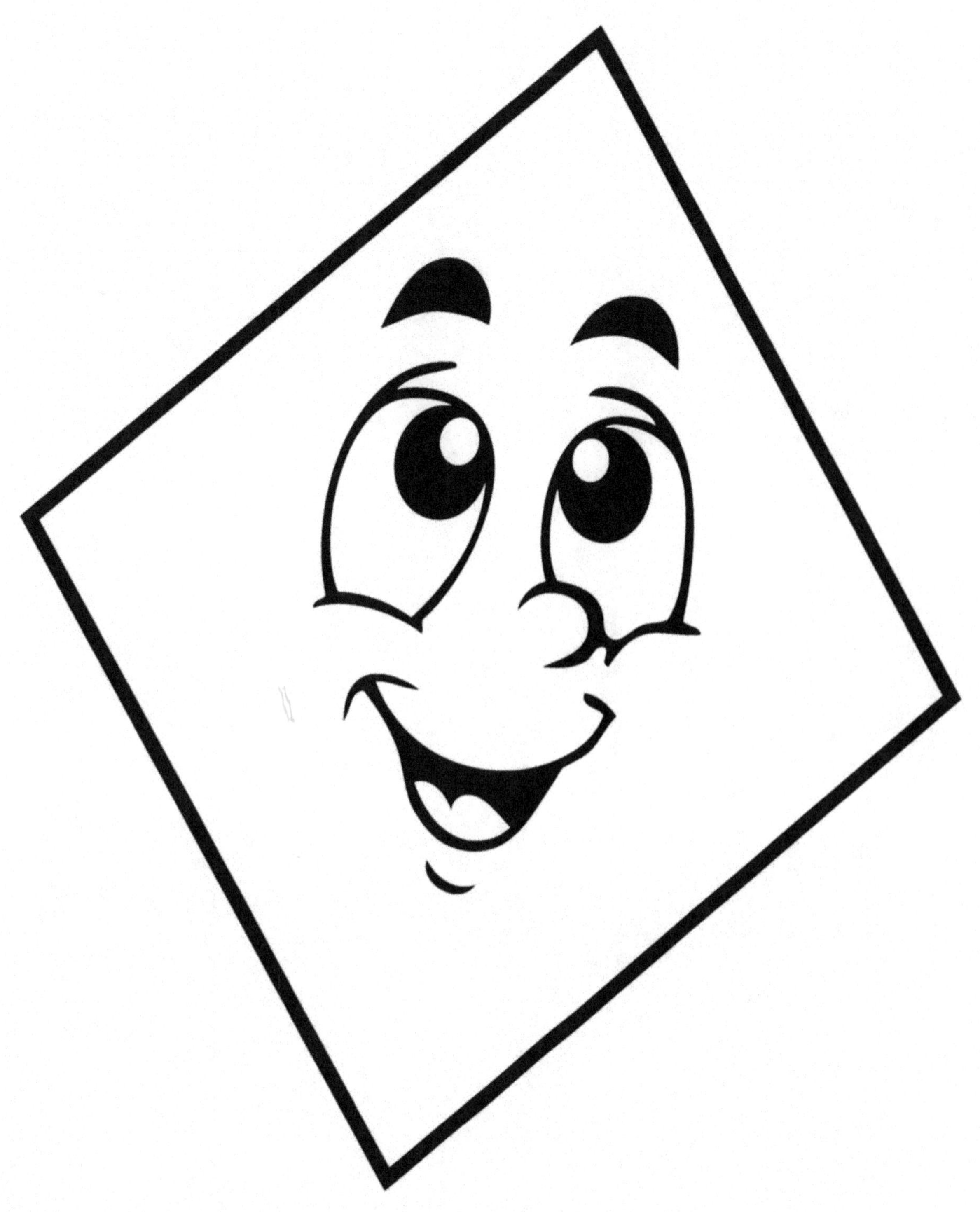

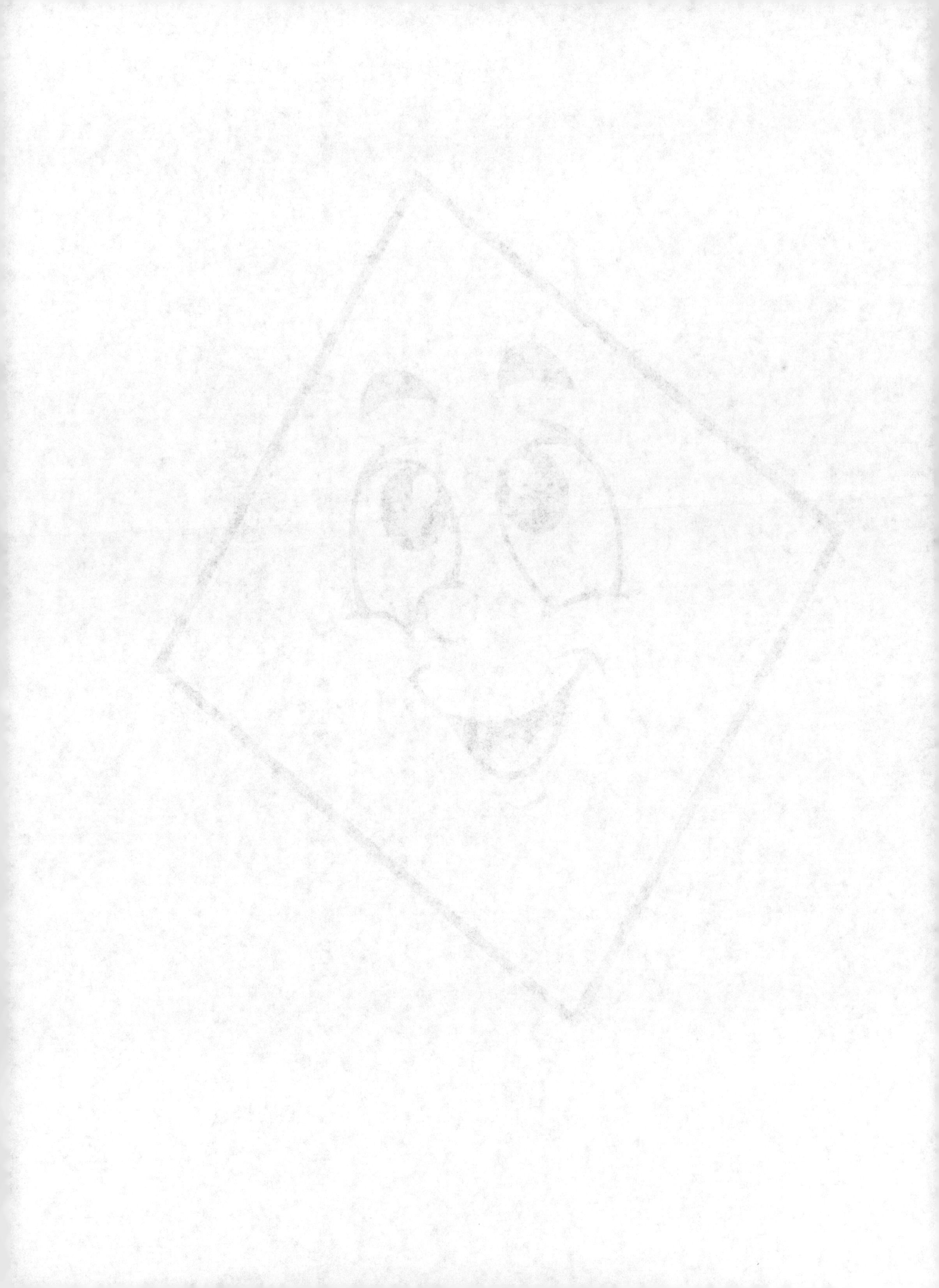